Old GRETNA

by
Rhona Wilson

The priest, Thomas Johnston, outside Gretna Green's 'Old Blacksmith's Shop'. However convenient for runaway couples from England, Gretna's marriage facilities did not please everyone and many local people were outraged by their existence. The anonymous minister who wrote Gretna's entry in the *Statistical Account of Scotland*, published in 1793, devoted an appendix to his feelings about John Paisley, although his remarks served to mythologise the man as much as denounce him: 'He is a fellow without literature, without principles, without morals and without manners.' Furthermore, the minister complained, many outsiders thought that the ceremonies were carried out by regular clergymen but in fact the village's official minister married an average of just seven couples a year in the early 1790s.

© Stenlake Publishing, 1999
First published in the United Kingdom, 1999,
reprinted 2012
by Stenlake Publishing Ltd,
01290 551122
www.stenake.co.uk

ISBN 9781840330670

By the early 1830s, the twenty ton Lochmabenstane was the sole survivor of an oval of whin or moor stones which may have been the remains of a druidical temple. The stones must have been moved some distance since only red or white sandstone is found in Gretna parish. Whatever its original purpose, the Lochmabenstane is part of Scottish civil history as it was used as a site for criminal trials. It is mentioned in documents dating as far back as 1398 when it was spelled as 'Clockmabenstane'. There are several theories as to where the stone's name derives from. Suggestions that it is linked with the town of Lochmaben have been dismissed and some think that it comes from the Gaelic 'cloch' meaning stone and 'mailan' meaning bunch or cluster. Others think it was named after the sixth or seventh century warrior called Mabon who was reputedly killed in a battle near the parish of Ruthwell. The Lochmabenstane can still be seen today on the shore at Gretna at the end of Old Graitney Road.

INTRODUCTION

Gretna Green's international fame as the home of runaway marriages stems from England's Marriage Act of 1754. Marriage amongst the Sassenachs, originally merely a civil affair, had become more of a religious ceremony by the mid-sixteenth century and the new act imposed further restrictions; the age of consent was fixed at twenty-one, the banns had to be read out in advance of the wedding date, and two witnesses were required to make the marriage legal. The act made it much more difficult for illicit marriages to take place and Gretna, the first village across the border, was in a prime position to take advantage of under-age English youngsters in a hurry to get married. Demand for Gretna's services was immediate and in the same year that the act was passed Joseph Paisley took advantage of the new commercial opportunities. He became one of Gretna's most notorious 'priests', shrugging off the outraged disapproval of the parish's ministers for the next sixty years.

Despite the village's current dependency on tourism, it developed in a conventional way over the eighteenth and nineteenth centuries. The Union of 1707 brought stability to the border region, allowing its inhabitants to develop their agricultural economy around crops such as oats, potatoes and barley. Combined with a little fishing, farm labouring was the means by which most of its population of around 1,800 made a living in the 1790s. Improvements to estates such as land enclosure and the use of fertilisers like lime helped to triple the parish rental value over a 25 year period. In 1791 Sir William Maxwell brought modern manufacturing to Gretna by building Springfield village. Its five hundred strong population consisted mostly of hand-loom weavers and the village also brought about a change in the marriage market as it was much nearer the border than the established venues.

Just as the turnpike roads of the late 1770s had done, the arrival of the railways in the nineteenth century improved access to Gretna and irregular marriages continued to thrive due to these improved communications until the amendment of the Marriage Act in 1856. Lord Brougham, who had taken full advantage of Gretna's opportunities at the time of his own elopement, introduced a 21-day residency clause for those hailing from outwith Scotland and the mayor of nearby Carlisle sent a petition to parliament supporting the bill. Instantaneous marriages came to an end when the bill was passed and the trade declined until the fledgling tourism industry revived it in the early twentieth century.

The First World War brought massive changes to the district. In 1916 it was chosen by the government as the site of a munitions works to produce cordite explosives. Almost overnight a gigantic township to house its operatives sprung up thanks to the efforts of an astonishing 30,000 labourers. Unfortunately, leisure facilities were hardly a priority and the township's inhabitants, like those in other hastily built munitions plants, turned to alcohol in their attempts to relieve the monotony. 'Drunkenness among munitions workers,' thundered Prime Minister David Lloyd George, 'is doing more to damage the war effort than all the German submarines put together.' A State Management Scheme took over the sale of alcohol in the Gretna area in 1916 and was so successful in its aims that Sir Arthur Conan Doyle, in his role as war propagandist, was able to laud the township as a 'miracle of efficiency' in November of the same year.

Today, Gretna is a dormitory town and very much a tourist attraction. Every summer thousands flock to the 'Old Blacksmith's Shop'; in 1996, 45% of Dumfries and Galloway's 900,000 annual visitors made a visit to this attraction. Some tourists stay just a few hours as part of a coach trip while others arrive as part of a marriage party. Local council efforts to spread the benefit of tourist spending power have not always been appreciated, however. For example, the decision to build a registry office in Gretna township in the 1980s was much protested against by villagers who pointed out that there was no historical basis for doing so. It would seem that despite Gretna's chequered past the villagers are still proud of their heritage.

The old Toll Bar – reputedly the 'first house in Scotland'. A feature of modern Gretna Green is the large number of so-called 'old smithies' and other marriage venues, although this is historically accurate because many priests vied for the business available. John Paisley was one of the first on the scene in 1754 and he quickly developed a formidable reputation. Weighing 25 stones, he could bend iron pokers and straighten horse shoes with his bare hands. There is little doubt that he was an alcoholic and one story tells of how he and a friend drank ten gallons of cognac over a two and a half day period. Marrying an average of sixty couples per year with an annual income of £945, he could certainly afford to. 'Is it not a reflection on the good sense and discernment of the Nobles and Gentry of England . . . to suffer themselves to be imposed upon, and their pockets to be picked, by such miscreants?' implored the minister in the *Statistical Account*.

The road north from Gretna to Springfield is now the A74. Although it was possible for marriage to be a purely civil ceremony in Scotland, by the eighteenth century convention dictated that it be carried out in a church, with the consent of parents, and with the banns read out beforehand. As a result, a dim view was generally taken of irregular marriages. Marriage ceremonies were only officially recognised from the twelfth century and some local customs continued to reflect a variety of interpretations of the rite that existed since ancient times. In Langholm in Dumfriesshire, for example, the annual holiday of the Handfasting Fair was an opportunity for couples to enter into a one year trial marriage. The following year they could choose to marry properly or split up, with any child becoming the responsibility of the partner who chose to leave. Such practices were likely motivated by practical reasons. For example, the tacksmen who worked the land needed large families to assist them and a fertile wife was a necessity. Trial marriages were thus a way of ensuring a woman could bear children.

The white building at the near end of the road is Springfield Farmhouse which still stands, while the two-storey white house on the right, the Maxwell Arms, has since been demolished and replaced by a dwelling house. Springfield village was an improving venture built by Sir William Maxwell in 1791 in order to develop his estate. The streets were fifty feet wide and the houses were all built from local freestone and blue slate. By 1793 there were about forty dwellings and each owner was allocated between four and six acres of land on a nineteen year lease. The main inhabitants were weavers, who were soon to benefit from the boom years of the Napoleonic Wars when their skills would be much in demand for weaving blankets and material for uniforms. The village had the advantage of being near a river and Sarkfoot Port and seemed to have a prosperous future ahead of it. The *Statistical Account* records, 'there seems to be little doubt of this village becoming a considerable place in a short time.'

Springfield's position just over the border gave it an edge over its rivals in the marriage business. One who took advantage was Lord Erskine, whose wedding at the village's Queen's Head Hotel in 1816 is a good example of the outlandish events which could occur in the area. In a startling role reversal the 66 year old Lord Chancellor eloped to escape the disapproval of his children. After the death of his first wife in 1805, he took up a mistress called Sarah Buck who bore him two children out of wedlock. The children of his first marriage were angry with this potential threat to their inheritance and pressurised him to not to marry Sarah. Lord Erskine declined the advice and, arriving at Gretna disguised as a woman, was married to his mistress by the priest David Lang. In true runaway style, his son, the Honourable Thomas Erskine, rode up to take his father to task just as the ceremony was completed. Still in existence is a pane of glass from the Queen's Head on which Lord Erskine scratched his signature during his stay.

This house in Springfield was formerly an inn kept by Thomas Little who was known to villagers as 'Tam the Piper'. The man standing in the doorway is Peter Dixon, the inn's priest. This postcard was sent to 'Annie' by her sweetheart, 'Alf', in 1917. Possibly, Alf was a soldier leaving for France as it reads: 'My dear Annie, just a few lines dearest to let you know that I am doing OK and in the best of health. Hoping you are likewise. Well darling, I am sending you a table centre along with this postcard and hoping you will receive it alright. I would like to give you something better but never mind dearest – wait till I get back and I will give you myself, that is if you will have me. This postcard is of a house in Scotland where the runaway marriages used to be held long ago. Well dear little sweetheart this is all the time I have so I will say goodbye. I remain your ever loving boy, Alf.'

THOMAS JOHNSTONE, LATE GRETNA GREEN PRIEST.   6825Y. JV.

The priest Thomas Johnstone, photographed in 1909. The legend of the blacksmith who married couples over the anvil seems to have no basis in fact. Priests came from a variety of backgrounds and were simply motivated by their need to make money quickly and easily. One of the best known was David Lang, a nephew of Joseph Paisley, who was born in 1755. A victim of the press-gangs, he had an exciting if unasked for career in the navy during which the ship he was serving on was captured by John Paul Jones, founder of the American navy. He managed to escape when Jones attempted a raid on the Solway Firth, an area Lang knew well, and thereafter he settled down to marrying for a living. Lang's premises were at the eastern end of Springfield village which meant that not only did he catch customers before they got to Gretna Green, they were more likely to pay handsomely for his services since they could afford to travel by carriage along the main road. Lang was one of the first Gretna priests to keep records of the marriages he carried out.

D. R. Macintosh

Proprietor of Gretna Hall, who performs runaway Marriages Over the Anvil.

David Ramsay Macintosh, the priest of Gretna Hall. According to the notes on the back of this photograph, he married 139 couples between 1 January 1938 and 6 August the same year. During his career he was rivalled by Richard Rennison who was the priest at the Old Blacksmith's Shop between 1927 and 1940. A former rabbit catcher, he claimed to have married 5,147 people including the nine foot Dutchman, Jan Van Albert.

Gretna Hall was built in 1710 by Colonel James Johnstone, supposedly for his new bride Isabella. Both this date and the Johnstone motto, 'Beware, we are prepared', appear above the entrance door. The Colonel's son James inherited the house when his father died in 1730 and sixty years later it passed to the Earl of Hopetoun. It was under the latter's ownership when it was converted for use as an inn around 1793. Eventually, the hall started offering marriage services and gained a profitable share in the business. Being an obviously grander venue than the cottages in Springfield village, it attracted an upper class clientele, some of whom could afford to pay as much as £10 for the ceremony. 1,134 marriages appear on its register.

Prince Charlie's Cottage and the parish church at Gretna Green, 1928. John Linton, the nineteenth century inn keeper at Gretna Hall, acted only as a witness to marriages before taking up the mantle of priest himself. He became known as 'The Bishop' on account of his scruples, previously unencountered in Gretna, against marrying 'drunks and reprobates'. The hall was sold when the estate was broken up in 1889 and eventually came into the hands of David Ramsay Macintosh in 1938. Macintosh converted the stables at the back into a 'smithy', signposted as 'The Original Marriage House', and won the right to keep it there in the resulting court battle with the proprietor of the Old Blacksmith's Shop, Hugh Mackie. Macintosh won when it was proved that his establishment owned the oldest marriage anvil in Gretna. Gretna Hall is still standing, although it has been extensively extended, and visitors can see its Bridal Chamber and diamond scratched window panes.

PRINCE CHARLIE'S COTTAGE, GRETNA GREEN.

Bonnie Prince Charlie's army passed through Gretna on their retreat from England in 1745. The Young Pretender is believed to have spent a night in this cottage which is now a guest house. Rev. Gatt, Gretna's minister at the time of the army's visit, recorded in the church minutes that he took the precaution of retiring to an isolated farmhouse before its arrival. This cottage was once two separate buildings and is now a guest house.

Kirkcroft, the white building on the left, was originally Gretna's post office. Public interest in Gretna was particularly high in the mid-nineteenth century for several reasons. The arrival of the railways, like the turnpikes built in 1777, made travel to the village easier and the resulting increase in the number of irregular marriages offended Victorian sensibilities. Gretna's minister of 1834 demanded that this kind of marriage be outlawed, proposing that the General Assembly send a petition to parliament in support of this request. In 1852 Charles Dickens visited the village to write an article about the phenomenon and the mayor of Carlisle called a public debate to discuss the issue in 1856. Carlisle's annual Hiring Day Fair often ended in hasty drunken marriages at Gretna Green and the debate resulted in the town sending a petition to parliament in support of Lord Brougham's 21-day residency clause.

The cottages at Sarkside, Gretna. Henry's shop was located where the two children are standing.

Old Sark Bridge spans the border between England and Scotland. Sark Toll can be reached from Gretna by travelling along the lane opposite the Queen's Head Inn which was known as 'the new road' when it was opened around 1830. David Lang, the tollkeeper, had a great opportunity to exploit the marriage market because he was nearer the border than the Springfield priests. A later priest, John Murray, built the Sarkbank Hotel (now the Gretna Chase Hotel) on the English side of the border around 1855. This proved a badly timed moved as he hoped to provide an alternative to Gretna Hall for upper class runaways but was stymied by Lord Brougham's amendment to the Marriage (Scotland) Act which happened around the same time. This required couples from outwith Scotland to prove a three week residency period in the country before marriage and severely cut back on the number of Gretna elopements.

Sark Bridge Farm Hotel. Although tourism is currently Gretna's main industry, in the past the inhabitants made a living through agriculture, fishing and weaving. Wages were supposedly high for ordinary farm labourers because of Gretna's proximity to more salubrious places such as Cumberland, but despite the fact that a 'stout young man' could earn up to £4 10s at the Spring harvest, families still found it difficult to make ends meet. To counteract this women were expected to work during harvests and hay time and also spin cotton, the latter occupation bringing in around 1s per week.

16

The Union Jack Hotel. In the early 1830s Gretna's weaving community was left poverty stricken mainly because the end of the Napoleonic Wars had left too many of them chasing too little work. At that time the parish weavers were employed by Messrs Dickson and Ferguson of Carlisle and worked a twelve to fourteen hour day, six days a week. The average number of parishioners on the poor roll was thirty with the heritors meeting Gretna's minister once a year to inspect it. Parishioners of the 1830s wanted the heritors to undergo a legal assessment to ensure they paid a certain amount each year but this eventuality was held off by the 'firmness of the kirk session'. Charity was frowned upon so self-help savings schemes such as the Friendly Society of Kirkpatrick-Fleming and Graitney (set up around the 1750s), which provided a small income in the event of members losing work due to illness, were a much more acceptable solution.

Gretna's railway station was opened in the mid-nineteenth century and became the means by which many runaway couples arrived at the village. Priests touting for business at the station became such a problem that the Station Master banned them from the platforms.

Scotch Express Disaster near Carlisle.

The seeds of the disaster were sown in a private arrangement between Tinsley and Meakin. Tinsley was due to start work at 6.00 a.m. but caught a lift on a local train which arrived in Quintinshill at around 6.30 a.m., his colleague covering for him in the meantime. Once he arrived his usual practice was to copy down details of the train movements between 6.00 and 6.30 am, which he got from Meakin, to make it look like he had made his official start time. On the morning of the disaster not only was Meakin in the signal box with Tinsley, but also two brakesmen from goods' trains, so there was ample opportunity for distractions. Meakin's main error occurred when he shunted the local train onto the main line without placing rubber collars over the signal levers to act as a warning and reminder that it was there. Hutchinson, the fireman from the local train, went on trial along with Tinsley and Meakin because he had failed to ensure that this had been done.

Immediately after the collisions, fire broke out. Hot coals from the engine of the troop train set alight the wooden carriages and the flames were fed by gas for the train's lighting supply. Despite vain attempts to quell the flames with water from the tanks of two goods trains and by syphoning water from a nearby stream, the inferno raged for 24 hours with devastating results. Once it was extinguished, 82 bodies were unrecognisable and fifty were never traced at all. There were rumours that some men trapped by the wreckage were shot by their officers to save them from burning to death. Although the Carlisle Fire Brigade was sent news of the disaster just after 7 a.m., it failed to reach the scene for three hours. Some have claimed that the young man who motorcycled to town to give them the message was laughed out of the building.

In the aftermath of the disaster, a roll call mustered a straggling row of just fifty troops. The exact number of men who died is unknown because the battalion's documentation was lost in the fire. Eight people died in the express train with 54 injured and two passengers died on the local train. A fourteen year old boy was run over and killed by a motor cycle while travelling to the scene of the disaster. Locals, railwaymen and survivors did what they could to help and amputations were carried out, 'with razor blades and bayonets' according to one commentator, to free men from the wreckage. The injured were taken to medical facilities in Carlisle.

Ambulance Train, Gretna Green Railway Disaster, May 22, 1915.

Most of the troops had come from Leith and Musselburgh and their funerals were held in Rosebank Cemetery two days later. At the inquiry into the disaster, the Accident Inspector, Colonel Druitt, made several recommendations to ensure that the fire which killed so many had less chance of doing so in future accidents. He advised that electric lighting should be used in place of gas and carriages should be made of steel instead of wood whenever possible. His report also stated that trains should carry equipment to deal with potential disasters, such as fire extinguishers and tools to cut through wreckage.

24

Express Engines Wrecked, Gretna Green Railway Disaster. May 22, 1915

Meakin and Tinsley were arrested for the Coroner's inquest at Carlisle and stood trial in September 1915 at Edinburgh High Court. The jury took less than ten minutes to return a guilty verdict; Meakin was imprisoned for one and a half years, Tinsley for three. Some thought the sentences were harsh since, regardless of the consequences of their actions, their records were clean and their awful carelessness and forgetfulness were mistakes made by many other signalmen. Both had nervous breakdowns during the course of their sentences.

The disaster at Quintinshill never had the public profile of many lesser incidents because it happened during wartime and reporting of it was restricted. Its file at the Scottish Records Office will be unavailable to the public until 2015. Two memorials to the troops were built at Rosebank Cemetery and one was erected at Gretna Tourist Office in the mid-1990s by the Scottish Area of the Western Front Association. Although the site of the disaster is half a mile away, many locals felt this was an inappropriate venue. Today, little trace of Quintinshill remains. The signal box was pulled down in the early 1970s and the loops had been removed by the 1990s.

The First World War transformed Gretna forever, as can be seen by the hoards of munitions operatives emerging from Gretna township Station in this postcard from the period. During the early stages of the war the parish was chosen as the site for a munitions plant after *The Times* newspaper printed an article blaming Britain's poor progress in the war on the lack of explosives available. Gretna's qualifications included its access to a railway service, its water supply and the protection of the nearby Cheviot, Penine and Cumbrian mountain ranges which made bombing attacks less likely. The township and factory, stretching nine miles from Dornock to Gretna, went up in record time. Thirty thousand construction workers arrived almost overnight, with 600 wagon-loads of building materials arriving each day. Tricky questions were asked of the Ministry of Munitions about the plant's construction once the war was over. It was claimed that, even while the township was being built, subsidence was occurring because it was built on peat foundations.

Gretna township's 20,000 operatives began arriving in June 1916. Brick houses were built for factory officials while married navies were allocated wooden huts and single people had to make do with a place in one of the dormitories. The first batches of cordite explosive left the township, code-named 'Moorside', in August 1916. Production of cordite was potentially difficult because it required large quantities of acetone, an organic solvent. This was used to transform the explosive components of gun-cotton and nitro-glycerine into a dough which could then be moulded into 'cords'. As acetone was difficult to obtain in large enough quantities, a combination of ether and alcohol was considered the next best thing and 'Moorside' had its own ether and glycerine distilleries.

STAFF CLUB, GRETNA TOWNSHIP.

It's unlikely whether this sedate looking staff club (now Hunter's Lodge) would have attracted the plant's early occupants. A newspaper report of the time declared that the township was comprised of 'socially, elements not easily managed' and their behaviour resulted in the state taking control of the production and sale of alcohol in Gretna. Direct contemporary references to what went on in the township at the time are difficult to find because of war censorship; one newspaper journalist remarked that 'one must of necessity, in times like these, be diffident of enlarging on such matters . . . ' The stories came out afterwards, however. On pay day Carlisle was inundated with Gretna munitions workers attempting to get drunk. The only train to the town arrived five minutes before closing time so the workers bribed the engine driver to arrive faster. An arrangement was also made with the owner of the Banstead Bar to ensure that he had hundreds of whisky shots prepared for their arrival.

CINEMA, GRETNA TOWNSHIP.

The cinema on Central Avenue. A similar state management scheme was implemented at the submarine base at Dingwall and at both there and Gretna there were dramatic drops in the number of court appearances. In the four weeks before Gretna's new licensing laws came into effect there were 1,485 convictions per week for drunkenness in Scotland as a whole; this dropped to an average of 947 once state management was in place and was around the 237 mark by November 1918. Irish construction navvies were the group generally blamed for drunkenness and lawlessness at Gretna and nearby Annan, which was ironic because one of the township's advantages in terms of labour needs was its proximity to the Irish sea crossing at Stranraer. Wages for these men were considered sky high compared to normal rates of pay but there was little to spend them on, besides alcohol, while the moorland site was under construction.

Portion Of Gretna Township.

Although set up in extreme circumstances, state management of alcohol in Gretna district lasted for 55 years. The Central Liquor Control Board's first step was to abolish all grocers' licences in the area. Many labourers involved in the construction of the township were housed in Annan and the village's streets were completely congested on weekend nights with workers out looking to spend their wages. The village's off-licences were all closed bar one and the sale of spirits was banned in public houses in Springfield and Kirkpatrick-Fleming by June 1916. The Globe pub in Annan was closed down at the end of July and reopened as a non-licensed restaurant and Gracie's Banking Tavern was opened in the town with its own restaurant, bowling green and cinema facilities. However, it was reported in 1917 that the cinema was '. . . not yet fully appreciated by the mass of labourers.'

Fire Station & Hose Tower, Cretna Township.

Gretna township's fire station still stands on Central Avenue. Gracie's Banking Tavern is a good example of the techniques used by the Liquor Control Board to control alcohol consumption. The tavern sold only beer and wine – no spirits – and there was no bar; all alcohol was carried by waitresses to tables which meant that people were more likely to combine drink with food. This concept was loosely based on Sweden's Gothenburg system which attempted to encourage moderate drinking by providing leisure facilities and food in addition to alcohol. At the tavern there were draughts, dominoes, newspapers and billiard tables but, although convictions due to drunkenness halved because of the lack of alcohol outlets, labourers did not gravitate solely to Gracie's. A *Glasgow Herald* report from April 1917 stated that the tavern was only busy on Saturday nights and other licensed houses were no less busy as a result because Scottish working men liked to drink spirits.

Mary Queen of Scots Dinning Hall

G. Earsman Gretna

Despite the severity of the measures taken at Gretna there were some protests in parliament from MPs who felt that they didn't go far enough. In April 1917, Mr Molento, MP for Dumfriesshire, pointed out that £60,000 worth of whisky had been brought into Gretna in the previous two months and that this had a knock-on effect since the alcohol was produced using important food materials such as grain. There were further protests after the King's visit to Gretna Tavern later that year because afterwards the royal monogram was put on the tavern chairs. The visit was a mark of appreciation for the 800 tons of cordite produced each week in 1917.

Thousands of women were employed at Gretna in the difficult and dangerous job of producing cordite. The local recruitment officer was Miss Pullinger of Crocketford and she helped bring in girls from Newcastle, Wales and Ireland. There were strict rules regarding uniforms since the explosive was produced by several unstable processes. No buttons were allowed on clothing or hairgrips in the girls' hair because an explosion could result if either of these got into the gun-cotton. Workers would be fined by one of the 'lady police' if caught with an offending item on their person. One woman died in an explosion when some dirt got into the mixture and her colleagues were given the following day off so that the place could be cleaned up. Altogether, 300 munitions workers lost their lives due to factory explosions during the First World War.

34

H.M. Factory Gretna, Staff Department.

Those working in the staff department were somewhat better off than the girls on the factory floor. Conditions in both the hostels and the factories were harsh, the cold alone being the cause of much hardship. Bedrooms in the dormitories had no doors and floors would ice over when they were being washed in the winter. Indoors, towels had to be heated before use while outdoors rats scampered about the girls' feet as they worked. Other health hazards included fumes from the chemicals they worked with. It was possible to get drunk on the cordite fumes but the consequences could be far worse than that; one Gretna worker had to have her teeth removed after they rotted due to exposure to acid fumes. It is not possible to tell who is who in this photograph but perhaps readers may be able to help identify them. The names are Alice Baird, E. Blackburne, E. Brown, J. Young, Winifred Dawson, M. Johnstone, J. Braemner, R. J. Robinson, Alfred Lindsay, R. M. Vend, W.C. Donaldson, J. G. Rennie and I. M. Dawson.

The Gretna Girls.

THE Gretna girls are here, lads—Gretna women, too,
    From sweet sixteen to sixty, seeing "Tommy"
        through :
Girls from Scottish hillsides, strong in health and vigour,
Girls from desk and counter, neat in style and figure ;
" Hinnies " from the Tyneside, Geordie's bonnie bairns—
At Whitley Bay they'll show them what the Gretna lassie
        earns ;
Jolly girls from Yorkshire—tha' knows th' sort Ah mean—
"Gradely" girls from Lancashire with eyes devoid of green.
Sure ! there's winsome Irish colleens, with lashes black
        as sloes,
They've " stuck it " all the winter through Border frost
        and snows.
Hear them in the morning, singing through the streets,
With their little nose-bags full of grub——and sweets.
" There's a long, long trail a-winding " to the stations
        every day,
To " keep the home fires burning " for laddies far away.
" When Irish eyes are smiling," Scotch and English are
        not sad,
They all sing " Tipperary " as though they had gone mad.
Pouring from the hostels, happy, gay, and bright—
Week-day, Sunday, holiday, morning, noon, and night.
Pink cheeks from the country, pale cheeks from the town,
A month or two at Gretna turns them ruddy brown.
Rosy cheeks or white cheeks, each is doing her best
To help our gallant warriors fighting East and West.
Write and tell your soldier pal, it's sure to cheer his heart
To know the girl he left behind so nobly plays her part.
If he hears about her " clicking," tell him not to worry,
When he returns the " home reserves " will " dismiss "
        in a hurry.
So three cheers for the Gretna lasses ! give another three,
They're doing their bit right heartily to keep old Britain
        free.
" Tom " and " Jack " when they come back will show
        appreciation
By " joining up " with girls who are a credit to the nation.

Copyright, 1917, by A. BURNS, *Carlisle.*

Although this postcard presents a rather sentimental view of the Gretna women, its production does indicate the level of popular respect the female workers gained by their contribution to the war effort.

GIRL'S READING ROOM, INSTITUTE, GRETNA TOWNSHIP.

Gretna munitions plant was operational for just two years before it began to be wound down. A newspaper article of December 1917 reported that approximately 1,500 women would be discharged from their duties in the run up to Christmas. It is obvious from many newspaper reports of the time that munitions work was not considered to be 'real' employment for the girls and that the experience was merely a temporary interlude in their lives. One journalist blithely commented that after the war the women would be returning to their home towns to set up households while others would return to the jobs they had previously held as domestic servants or in the fishing industry. Cutbacks in the number of employees took place continually, reducing the figures from 20,000 to only 3,000 by the Armistice.

GRETNA TOWNSHIP, (West).

J.G.Clayton
Gretna

In August 1919 plans to close the factory were made public – all officials would be dispensed with and only sufficient employees would be retained to maintain the factory buildings. Waltham Abbey munitions plant in England was ear-marked for conversion into the national gunpowder factory but Gretna's future was less certain. The Ministry of Munitions tried to downplay any potential unemployment by pointing out that there was a labour shortage in Carlisle with many firms in the town having to import workers from the east coast. Alternative industries were suggested such as the proposal that the works should be transformed into a railway wagon construction depot, but this angered wagon builders who felt that their livelihood would suffer if they had competition from a nationalised industry.

Access to the beach near Gretna township is now restricted by the MOD. By October 1919 the Ministry of Munitions was going to rather desperate lengths to save money, some of which landed it in court. In January 1920, 142 operatives at Gretna brought a complaint about their wages before Sheriff Fyfe. Since October of the previous year, five shillings per week had been withheld from their pay packets on the justification that it represented a lodging allowance which the Ministry had decided they were no longer entitled to. In what was described as a 'unique, important and far reaching decision' by the *Glasgow Herald*, Sheriff Fyfe upheld their complaint, commenting that 'if they put a whisky label on a bottle of water that did not change it from a bottle of water to a bottle of whisky'. Despite this, he felt it unnecessary to impose a penalty on the Ministry.

INTERIOR BORDER HALL, GRETNA TOWNSHIP.

Dismissals at the factory continued throughout 1920 – there were just over 1,000 workers left by March – and relations between the Gretna community and the Ministry of Munitions were deteriorating rapidly. In November of that year the government created the concept of an 'Obligation Week' and asked local ministers to help them encourage an improvement in management-employee relations. The Gretna ministers sent a blistering reply to the Minister of Labour: 'You will agree that an employer who at this time withholds work unnecessarily from men who have served their country is lamentably deficient in his sense of the 'dear obligation' to which His Majesty refers.' The local clergy added that it was the 'duty' of the War Office to employ men to adapt the factory for a peace time requirement and of the Treasury to supply their wages.

40

St. Andrew's Church, Gretna.

The township's church. In February 1920 Sir John Rees proposed a motion in parliament to abolish all unnecessary restrictions, as he saw it, on the management of alcohol in the Gretna area. His speech took a far more flippant tone than would have been tolerated during war time. 'Carlisle,' he stated, 'is more than a sober town now; it is desperately dismal.' Rees quipped that he wouldn't serve government beer to his worst enemy and that the state should be wary of having too much control over its citizens in case it suffered a revolution *a la* the USSR. His attempt was in vain, however, and Lady Astor retaliated with the establishment view of the time, accusing Rees of being backward in his thinking. She argued that controlling the nation's drinking habits could only be good for the welfare of the community and national efficiency. Convictions for drunkenness in women had dropped by 80% during the war – did Sir John really want to return to the old world of pre-1914? The licensing restrictions in the Gretna district remained in place until the late 1960s.

Township School, Gretna.

J. G. Clayton Gretna.

A.S. Neill was headmaster of Gretna Public School during the First World War and was the author of *A Dominie's Log* which depicted life in the school and the village of Springfield. Neill was a forward thinking liberal whose unusual teaching methods got him into trouble with the Rev. John Stafford, a local councillor and member of Gretna Green School Committee. He didn't believe in either the use of corporal punishment or setting homework and tried to dispense with the rote learning which was a convention of the time. He also insisted that children work in reasonable conditions and outraged the school committee by closing the school one day when the building was too cold for comfort. Neill thought Stafford was a hypocrite and said so in his book, describing how Stafford preached the evils of drink but liked a drink himself and condemned those who swore but was well-known as a good source of a bawdy stories.

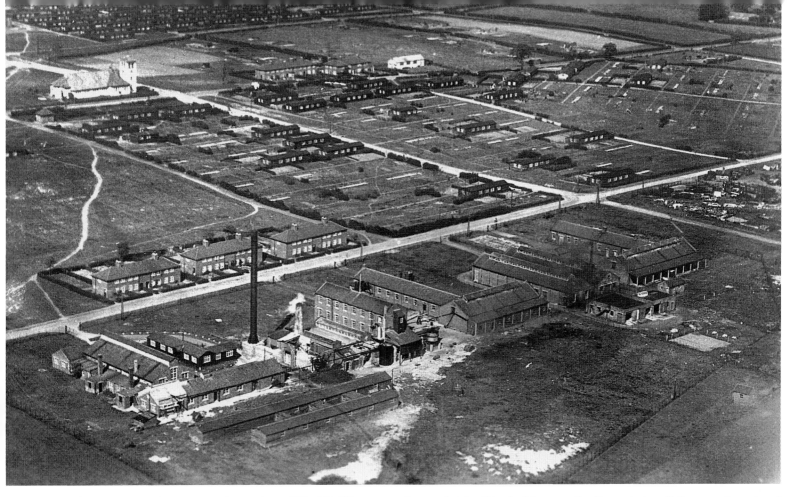

By June 1920 the munitions plant was costing an incredible £20,000 per month to maintain. The decision was finally made to sell the vacant asset and an advert was placed in *The Times* in September 1921. Messrs Tiffen & Sons and Messrs Gibbons & Sons of Carlisle were charged with cataloguing the bewildering array of lots which included stone, brick and steel constructed factories, ether and glycerine distilleries, a steam laundry, a bakery, the cinema, a hospital, houses, hostels and three farms. An auction at Carlisle County Hall was finally held in July 1924 and the works disappeared into the hands of private owners. Most of the factory buildings have been completely removed although a few ruins still remain.

Dornock Village near Annan.

Stretching for nine miles, Gretna munitions plant incorporated Eastriggs residential township and Dornock's largely industrial site. In the early 1830s, Dornock parish had a population of 730 with only 230 of these living in the village itself. Fishing, using stake or trap nets, was an important industry and the parish's catch was sold at the Carlisle market. Dornock was the landing site on the Scottish side of the ford across the Solway. Many people drowned in the ford trying to escape from the incessant border battles of the middle ages.

Post Office, Dornock

Many of the munitions plant's large factories, such as the glycerine distillery, were built in Dornock. Demolition of these after the war took a long time to complete and was in fact still ongoing by the start of the Second World War, by which time building began again to convert the factory into a storage depot for explosives. Only a few hundred people worked here during the early 1940s as opposed to the thousands during the First World War, but the work was a boon to the local economy which had been severely depressed since the 1920s. Today, Dornock is generally known as part of Eastriggs.

Central Hall, Eastriggs.

Ironically, Gretna's current role as a tourism centre dates from the early twentieth century when Scotland's right to conduct irregular marriages began to be undermined. In 1935 a committee was finally set up, headed by Lord Morrison, to investigate the centuries old profession. The main complaint it had to make when it reported its findings the following year was that couples were lax about officially registering their marriages since this required a journey to Dumfries with their witnesses. For the priests' part, they were charged with not enforcing the 21-day residency rule which meant that some of the marriages they were performing were just not legal. In order to stop what the report termed their 'commercialised robbery' it was proposed that a system of registry offices be set up throughout Scotland to conduct civil marriages and Gretna's opened in 1940.

The Green, Eastriggs.

Runaway couples were still drawn to Scotland, however, including the entrepreneur James Goldsmith and Isabel Patino, who eloped in 1953. Marriages in Gretna enjoyed a revival in the 1960s although the press coverage quickly became condemnatory about all the couples 'mooching around'. In 1970 the age of consent was lowered to eighteen in England meaning there was little need for couples to resort to elopement although mock marriages continue in Gretna to this day.

Tourism is now Gretna's mainstay, and although some have accused the town of a certain tackiness, tourists over the decades have included such luminaries as George V, Queen Mary, Prince Henry of Russia, David Lloyd George, King Hussain of Jordan and, most important of all, superstar Ken Dodd.